One Second of Light

Camille Hourtané

BookLeaf Publishing

Presentation by *BookLeaf Publishing*

Web: www.bookleafpub.com

E-mail: info@bookleafpub.com

ISBN: 9789357210218

First edition 2022

The Long Sleep

Darkness, sweet darkness, you beckon.
Your mantle hangs upon the shoulders of the
sky,
Will the stars ever shine upon your brow?
I am weary, treading paths to nowhere,
Bone-tired and sorrowed to my very heart.
Silky shadows darken my sights,
A restful breath stills my chest,
Can I resist your serene embrace?
The thought of light is unbearable,
It pierces my eyes and shrivels my thoughts.
Take me, take me away.
Bandage my wounds with obscurity,
Loosen my grip, hold me to your breast,
Give me peace.
I close my eyes. I let go.
Who knows how long I will sleep?

The Trickster

False love with a false heart
You cackle and rejoice and scheme
While I dance at your fingertips.
It is your smile,
Mouth dripping with honey,
As cold as Winter's breath,
As beautiful as Summer's end,
That paints truth over lies.
Beloved trickster,
How you tangled me in your cruel net.
You caught my wild roaming heart
And left it to suffocate on the shore,
Yet my breathless heart yearns for you.
You promised we would soar together
Empty promise of an empty heart.
Each day, I touch the end of despair,
And each day, I go deeper still.
My love, my false love,
My sweet, sweet trickster,
I clothe myself in your deceptions.
Our love is but a play,
A pantomime of misery,
And we act out our roles to perfection.
Whisper lies to my ears,
Mime lies for my eyes,

Caress lies onto my skin,
I will believe you with every heartbeat.
Make me cold and lovesick,
But do not take away your poisoned attentions.
Trickster, dearest to my heart,
I cry when you deceive me,
But I die when you leave.

The Trickster II

False love, how false your love.
How foul its perfume
How dissonant its song.
Your mouth is red with untruth.
You kicked my heart around as a toy,
Held it beneath your heel,
And devoured it with glutton appetite.
Prometheus of the unloved,
I near renounced my heart to you.
You offered my lies of comfort,
Like a warm cloak of thorns,
But your words turned sour,
As soon as the wind blew South.
Lovely trickster, vile deceiver,
Your forgeries erased the stars from my sky
But my star shines anew.
You willed to bend me,
To blind me with your mask of falsehood,
Yet I remain unbent and unmasked.
I bid you gone from my sight,
Poison tongue and cruel love,
You stain my heart no more.
I swam in the Lethe and banished your from memory,
Even the taste of your bitter love will fade.

Trickster, forgotten one,
I am free at last.
Swallow your lies,
My ear is deaf to your plea,
And my solitude is a gift of life.

About Horses

To ride a horse
Is to see the world through the eyes of birds and kings.
It is to near the horizon
And to dream up one being with two hearts.
What rider fears thunder
More fierce than the thunder of hooves?
What rider knows loneliness
With hay breath upon their neck?
What rider ignores the taste of freedom
When they have learned to swallow rush winds?
Wild soul, gentle mind,
Back so strong it can carry a burdened heart.
Swishing tail, proud snorting,
Dancer of earthy lightness in the sand of the arena.
How generous your nature,
To bend the neck and tame your strength,
To accept the hand and the heel,
To lend us your grace and to give us your heart.

Redemption

Let the rain fall on me,
Cleaning my skin from filth and rancour.
Do not shield me with your plastic umbrella.
A cold does not matter
If I am cured of my ailments and my obscurity.
Merely a runny nose, after shedding thousands
of tears.

Daydreamer

I have walked away in thought,
On the barely seen paths of my mind,
My feet followed the charts of the stars
entwined,
And the trails the green fields have wrought.
I yearn to flee to faraway lands and streams,
Realms where the prince marries the
shepherdess,
Ere twilight, through midnight, my soul finds
egress
On the fair pathways I tread in dreams.

The Cat

The cat, rope-dancer upon the roofs, drowses all
day in sun-spills.
But when night comes, he meanders between the
hot breaths of the sleeping city,
Chasing ghosts and lovers.
At daybreak, he comes back from his secret
meetings, whiskers stained with blood,
Settles on a silk pillow, closes his eyes agleam,
And purrs.

The horses dance

See the rhythm of their stride,
How they follow the hand that guide.
They bend the neck with arrogance,
They lift their knees with pride.
Full of lightness and elegance,
The horses dance.

Thirty Years

Thirty years is not enough.
Fifty years, a hundred years is not enough.
Would a lifetime even suffice?
I have loved you for thirty years
And I learn to love you every day still.

It's how your hand fits right in mine
How I am braced by your arms
How you turn my flaws into strengths
How you love these little bits of me
That I've been trying to hide away
How you give me your time and attention
How you are worthy of respect
How you look at me when I take off my clothes
How you look at me when I speak
How we share worry and joy
How I smile when you say my name
How you look when you're passionate.

Thirty years with you is not enough
To love you as you deserve
To be by your side
Thirty years is not enough
Or a lifetime, or another.

The Witch

They call me a witch,
But they should name me Fear,
Or Nightmare, or Deception.
I am the Devil's bride,
The temptress with a black heart,
The wielder of profane magic.
They say I ensnare heedless men,
I turn virtuous wives baren,
And I toy with the souls of the innocents.

Yet I wield no fear,
But the fear, the dread, the terror
They imagine in their own mind.
I have no magic,
But I know how to listen and learn,
From the gifts of Mother Nature.
I do not tempt men,
But the men who are tempted
By the urge of their own desires.

They give me blame
For their shame and their sin.
They make me the monster
That they cannot face in their own mirror.
They lock themselves

In conventions and pretence,
Hiding behind veneer and masks,
Yet they sneer at those
Who would escape from that cage.
Do they not say
That misery loves company?

I refuse that cage,
I am not in that company.
I am the weed, the wildflower,
That defaces their orderly planters.
I embrace who I am,
I know the power inside of me.
And I will not muzzle it
To please the powerless by will.
I will not blind myself
To suit those who chose to wear blinkers.

I will keep learning,
Even when they want me ignorant.
I will rejoice in my beauty,
Even when they want me subdued.
I will speak my mind,
Even when they want me silent.
I will stand tall,
Even when they want me bent.
I will wield my magic,
Even as they fear me.

I am the learned,
I am the woman,
I am the witch.

To my Grave

One day I will go to my grave,
It is the path we must all walk,
But on my last hour I will not balk,
I will leave with a sunny wave.

At the reckoning, I won't resist,
I will laugh with my last breath,
When she comes I will greet Death,
Go freely when she takes my wrist.

I do not discard my life lightly,
Nor do I want its end hasted,
But to live without a day wasted,
Is to be reborn daily.

Regret makes us linger in life,
Unfulfillment makes death sour,
But if we live ere our last hour,
Then we can leave without a strife.

Weep not for me, for I have lived,
I did not wait for my grave to flower,
To gather the roses at every hour,
On my behalf, do not be grieved.

I leave no regrets, no task undone,
No path untravelled, no dream forsaken,
If tomorrow I do not awaken,
Celebrate my life when I am gone.

Traitor

Traitor, renegade of depravity,
You're the devil embodied.
Tomorrow, your life will end
In broken bones and spilt blood
Your flesh will burn
And your screams will delight the righteous.

Traitor to your creed
I admit it without shame
Snake of a two-faced faith
You spew love through greeted teeth
Yet you embrace hate as a brother.
Speak not of broken bones
When you go limping like an old dog
Under the weight of your broken soul.

Traitor, guard your tongue,
You speak ill of the faith
You taint the ears of the virtuous
And you spit in the face of our creator.
You blaspheme without remorse
And I will rejoice in your death.

Can the words of a mortal man
Wound a creator?

You do not fear for the creator,
You fear those whom you bridle.
Guard the flock from reason,
Let them not hear my words,
Lest the flock grows teeth
And comes biting at the door of the shepherd.

Traitor, do you hear?
The executioner is on his way.
Soon you will do no more harm.
A blessed silence will fall upon your mouth.
Repent for your heresy
Or face the wrath of our creator.

Were I to live a thousand years
I couldn't do more harm than you.
Your creed wields fear but names it love,
You preach bent knees over warm embrace.
You vilify all that will not comply
And slay those who deny your authority.
You have no faith,
You only have thirst for power.

Traitor, your head is on the block.
Your neck is in the noose, your pyre is lit.
Your funeral is sung, your life is drained from
your bones
Watch me smile over your corpse
And guide my flock away from you

Forlorn, forgotten, I swipe away your ashes.

I part from you without regret
I escape your claws as I die.
You curse my name,
But soon others will whisper it in praise.
Watch my flesh burn
As it ignites so many hearts.
It is not death, it is rebirth
A reckoning is at hand.

Sleep

Sleep, my darling,
Sleep til morrow.
Feel slumber lighten your head
Lift the worry off your brow.

Today's doubts are gone
Have no fear of the day to come
Sleep until tomorrow
In the morning, your ache will be numb.

Fall into reverie
Feel your body drifting away
Let dreams erase your burdens
They carry you safely to a new day.

Warrior

Face me with a host of snarling demons,
Bathe me in lave, throw me in a brasier,
Assail me with the wrath of volcanoes,
And sear my skin with foul fire.
Spit your flames til my armour melts,
And still, I will not despair.

Hope is tethered to my spine
To hope is to have a taste of tomorrow
It sings that all torments will end
So frail, so frail,
Yet so strong it can withstand the firestorm
And birth a flower from the ashes of a scorched
land.

Send forth your army of darkness,
Hollow creatures that dwell in sin and obscurity,
Order them to claw at my eyes,
Bequest them to tear the flesh from my bones,
Drown me in vile eldritch shadows,
Yet my light will never be extinguished.

My soul is my guide
The spark that shines brighter than the sun.

What gold or temptation can compare to its light?
My path shimmers before my feet,
As clear as the break of an untainted dawn,
And my soul is forever unafraid.

Unleash your winter hordes,
Pierce my body with shards of ice,
Freeze my jaw until I cannot speak,
Bury me in the fury of an avalanche,
And break my limbs in a stampede of wintry beasts,
Yet my heart will never be hardened by frost.

Love guards me against sorrow and strengthens my arm,
It is the armour and the sword,
It is the rescued and the saviour,
Fierce, tender love, more precious than the treasure of a king,
I can halt the tears of a child,
And carry the sky on my shoulders.

One Second of Light

One second of light
Before an endless night
One flower, lone and slight
In a land of scorch and blight.

Feel the burn of the flame, pick up the pace,
Sleep til noon, feel winter's frost on your face.
Watch the stars, be heartbroken,
Remove the pebble from your shoe, learn you're
mistaken.
Sing along, watch how the trees grow,
Face the wind with tears in your eyes, curse at
the snow.
Say that word over and over again, accept
getting old,
Be gentle, watch your breath rise in the cold.
Embrace her, leave footprints in the sand,
Try strange walks, enjoy things that go as
planned.
Take a chance, turn your face to the sun
Count on your fingers, see who you can outrun.

One second of light
Lest we forget
One second of light

Is all we get

Journey

Hear, hear, the wind is calling,
At my feet, the path is unfurling,
The wilds push me out my door,
When will I see my home once more?

Hear, hear, the wind is blowing,
The seasons on the road ushering,
Picks up my hair, picks up my pace,
In mountains and meadows I leave a trace.

Hear, hear, the wind is hushing,
Soon the journey will be ending,
I will turn back, no longer roam,
I'll find my hearth, my house, my home.

Le Fluide des Mots

Les phrases sont des fleuves,
Les gouttes d'eau sont des mots qui se meuvent.
Les rochers sont des virgules,
Su r lesquelles les mots rebondissent et reculent.
Les points sont des barrages,
Que l'eau heurte et assaille avec rage.
Lorsqu'il s'ouvre, l'eau grandit,
Comme une grande majuscule que l'on écrit.
Les rivières coulent sous les ponts,
Comme les mots traversent les deux points.
Les écluses des bateaux,
Sont les parenthèses qui séparent les groupes de mots.
Comme les fleuves vont à la mer,
Les mots vont aux vers ou aux textes littéraires.

Cerf-Volant

Cerf-volant, acrobate du ciel,
Arlequin aux couleurs vives,
Qui sourit à ceux qui savent le voir,
Tandis que la voile ancrée au sol
Dessine des arabesques folles,
Pour l'imagination des enfants.

www.ingramcontent.com/pod-product-compliance
Lightning Source LLC
Chambersburg PA
CBHW051718130826
49812CB00034B/1236
9789357210218